THE HANDBOOK
FOR LEADERS

THE HANDBOOK FOR LEADERS

Provocative Proactive Productive

Leadership

Georges Philips

CONTENTS

ABOUT THE BOOK

The Handbook for Leaders has been designed to give you a broad view on exemplary practice for leadership.

Leadership principles will apply regardless of whether you are in private or public enterprise or working in the community and voluntary sector. This book will not only remind you of some key leadership issues but, more importantly, it will further enhance your thinking and develop your insight. You will, moreover, be furnished with practical tools in order to guarantee your leadership success. You will thus be provided with a foundation on which you can construct or consolidate your leadership skills.

The wisdom within *The Handbook for Leaders* will apply if you are on a trajectory toward a leadership role or if you already command an implicit leadership position.

PREFACE

The Handbook for Leaders has been written so that you can truly understand the contributory factors involved in becoming an exceptional, if not an extraordinary, leader.

If you are a leader you will inevitably attain one of three outcomes on your journey to the top. You will either perish, survive or thrive but for you to be successful you must thrive.

You may have a concept of your leadership function within your organization or your industry but your leadership role will be characterized by your capability, your motivation and your mindset and these factors should be implicitly understood if you are to thrive. Throughout *The Handbook for Leaders*, therefore, you will discover a myriad of suggestions and techniques for rendering yourself a cut above the competition.

As the lynchpin in your organization you must have a vision coupled with the ability to turn your vision into practical reality. You will also need to convincingly convey your visionary ideas to the wider workforce. You must, therefore, be able to communicate your purpose effectively to your team. You must also understand and inspire your team in order to bring your plans to fruition.

In *The Handbook for Leaders* you will learn the way in which you can adopt a simple approach to effectively leading people and to gaining a greater understanding of leadership mindset and characteristics. You will, therefore, ultimately evolve by drawing out the unique leader within you.

This book will not dwell on managerial complexities but will instead provide you with an insight into all the key leadership elements which, when successfully balanced together, will define you as a great leader.

Excellent leadership is not just about a technical ability or an expert knowledge. Your leadership skills and potential will be based on your understanding of the organizational world around you and the way in which your personnel can operate within it both intellectually and emotionally.

There will be opportunities and threats at almost every turn with which you will have to contend if you are to thrive. You will thrive in a climate in which you utilize all your processing power in order to derive benefit from any situation.

Start today. Lead with intelligence. Lead with presence. Lead to inspire.

Georges Philips

INSPIRATIONAL LEADERSHIP

If you want to go quickly, go alone.
If you want to go far, go together.

African proverb

Sprezzatura is a beautiful Italian word which denotes a combination of style, grace and class in connection with the ability to undertake a craft without visible effort.

Many great leaders have similar characteristics and possess an appeal which resembles enchantment. A great leader will naturally attract others in the pursuit of his dream.

Although the leadership path will nearly always be distinct and if you can continue your journey throughout your working career while others might feel complacent – you will certainly thrive.

LEADERSHIP PRINCIPLES

Successful leadership will always be underpinned by a number of key principles and these tenets will be explored throughout this book.

Perhaps you can begin your journey by asking yourself a simple question:

Why do I want to become a leader?

Now repeat this question until you have reached the core of your motivational drive. By acknowledging and understanding your personal motivation you will be able to embody the height which you wish to attain.

Your question-and-answer routine could look something like this:

QUESTION   Why do I want to become a leader?

RESPONSE   Because I want to be successful.

QUESTION   Why do I want to be successful?

RESPONSE   Because I want to do better for my family and myself.

QUESTION   Why do I want to do better for my family and myself?

RESPONSE   Because I want to provide a better future for us all.

QUESTION   Why do I want to provide a better future for us all?

RESPONSE   Because I will fulfil my responsibilities.

QUESTION   Why do I want to fulfil my responsibilities?

RESPONSE   Because I must.

QUESTION   Why must I?

RESPONSE   Because it is my responsibility.

The loop here will indicate that you have no further answers to ask and your final answer will suggest that your leadership motivation will be to fulfil your responsibilities.

You could, however, ask an entirely different question:

QUESTION   How will I feel when I fulfil my responsibilities?

RESPONSE   I will feel proud.

Now you can fulfil your personal ambition in leading your team or your organization in the direction of success and self-fulfilment.

Knowing what drives you personally will help to put things in perspective for you and will allow you to develop professionally over time if you remain sufficiently reflective. Any self-doubt or uncertainly will, by this means, be banished from your mind and you can then set your compass in the direction of success.

MANAGEMENT PRINCIPLES

You will need to understand your organization well enough to handle the challenges effortlessly and to seize the opportunities presented in varying social, economic and political climates.

You must understand your organization from a number of relevant perspectives so that you can cater for the needs of your stakeholders. You must, therefore, learn to visualize the perspective of each of your stakeholders and acknowledge the needs of numerous individual's crucial decision-making points.

You will usually have three principle stakeholder-groups whom you must consider.

Your enterprise

Your enterprise will consist of your employees and any shareholders.

Your employees

Your employees will consist of the wider workforce and any commissioned service areas.

Your consumers

Your consumers will consist of your customers and any other business sectors which you may serve.

You must satisfy all three groups of stakeholders to be successful in a leadership role. The challenge for you will be not only to satisfy each group but also to ensure that your balancing-act will meet the demands of your organization as a whole.

These stakeholder-groups will frequently be intertwined and interdependent on each other. If your interdependent groups can work in harmony then your success will be guaranteed. Your mission will be to homogenize these three stakeholder-groups effectively in order to generate congruence within your organization.

Fulfilling the needs of your stakeholder-groups may require you to be constantly vigilant so that you can nurture strong and mutually rewarding relationships. You will require an array of skills and techniques for this task and an ability to see things from many different angles with empathy.

Leadership, therefore, will not only demand some specific key competencies but you must also harness some essential personal qualities so that you can aspire to becoming an excellent leader.

LEADERSHIP FUNCTIONS

You should always aim to be provocative, practical and productive simultaneously.

Provocative leadership

Provocative leadership will demand that you are constantly alert to any opportunity which can nudge your personnel forward. You can continually seek improvement in income, productivity and profitability by being fully aware of any situation in progress and challenging your team to strive.

Your ability to be constructively provocative can generate exemplary results. You must, therefore, acquire the art of engaging with others provocatively. If you can believe in the capabilities of your personnel then each team-member will believe in himself.

Proactive leadership

It will be crucial that you can be proactive, engaging and able to participate fully in your leadership role so that you can enable and empower your personnel to perform to the best of their ability. If you do not fully engage proactively with your task you will become a passive saboteur of your own purpose.

When you are proactive you will constantly need to assess productivity until a culture of action-driven personnel has been firmly established in your organization.

Productive leadership

You will need to accurately monitor the performance of your personnel in order to ensure that each member of your team will be making a valuable contribution. You should, of course, be intolerant of passengers or bystanders in your team.

If you can assess the effectiveness and the efficiency of your team you will be in a better place to understand the capabilities of your organization as a whole and you can plan ahead accordingly.

You should be able to identify your team-members in terms of their attitudes and motivation to work. Perhaps you could ask yourself a number of questions in order to identify where your team-members sit on the suitability-for-employment scale:

Does your team-member have the necessary skills and does he want to get on?

Does your team-member want to engage fully in his work yet he lacks the relevant skills?

Does your team-member want to work but he only does enough to get by?

Does your team-member not want to work at all?

LEADERSHIP CONDUCT

You must draw a clear boundary between being a leader and having a personal life and being an individual in your own right.

You cannot afford to be over-familiar with your personnel – however much you may desire to treat a team-member as a friend. You should not allow your desire to be liked to cloud your judgement.

You should not, conversely, be detached from your team-members and you should always be approachable and take an interest in your personnel as human beings. You may need to challenge a trusted colleague, for instance, when the need arises and you should not shy away from your duty in this respect.

By being amiable and approachable yet detached and impartial you will be able to depend on your personnel to deliver your objectives. By knowing the characteristics, background and personality of each of your team-members and by taking a genuine interest in a team-member as a person you will know whom you can trust.

Always ensure, consequently, that you conduct a performance review for each of your personnel because this will provide you both with an opportunity to discuss progress and to iron out any problems. You should, of course, regard any performance review as an open two-way discussion.

KEY LEADERSHIP QUALITIES

*I never think of myself as an icon. What is in
other people's minds is not in my mind. I just
do my thing.*

Audrey Hepburn

OPTIMAL LEADERSHIP

You should understand the value of certain key leadership qualities in order to optimize your potential as a leader.

All exemplary leadership qualities are inherent within mankind. You should, therefore, seek to develop and to improve those professional qualities which will assist you in your mission. You will need to be strong, resilient and determined in this mission because you cannot afford to retreat every time you encounter any resistance to change within yourself.

VISION

If you can't communicate the vision in five minutes or less and get a reaction that signifies both understanding and interest, you are not done.

John P. Kotter

Your vision should be something so great that everyone will want to be a part of it. If you are a great leader you must dream big.

> *Who would have thought that when President J F Kennedy spoke at Rice University in September of 1962 that the USA would go to the moon and it would take just 84 months to accomplish?*

You must be a visionary and you must be driven towards the fulfilment of your vision. You will need to see the horizon and the direction in which you will be taking your organization and you should have a clear understanding of the journey ahead.

Without vision no-one will know where to aim. Unless you have a clear vision and a definitive mission statement which fits with the desired outcome you will be unlikely to achieve much and, in some instances, you may even regress. A powerful vision will be imperative if your organization is going to make progress.

You should establish a clear and overarching vision for your organization. Without this foresight you will engender a lack of direction, a weak culture and no critical path for success. You must thus put as much emphasis as possible on communicating your vision to your personnel so that they can clearly understand the way in which they will fit into your concept and what contribution they will be expected to make.

Your task will be to create the vision and the mission statement and then support your personnel to make it happen. You should, therefore, be able to present a solution to any problems which your personnel cannot overcome. Your vision and your insight into any potential difficulties will empower your team and will generate confidence.

It will be essential for you to formulate some tangible objectives for your organization in order to accomplish your vision. If you are unable to create the big picture you can do something which can work just as well. You will simply need to have a broad sense of what you want to happen in your organization as an outcome.

You may require help when formulating your vision so that your team can understand the journey which you are planning. Your vision should be clear and understandable. You do not want to lead short-sighted personnel and any myopia should be almost impossible if you are serious about turning your vision into a reality.

Not everyone in your organization will be able to perceive your grand vision. For some people it will not always be possible to see the big picture. It may be unnecessary, or even impossible, for an individual to see an image in panoramic high-definition colour. That person, however, will not be incapable of having a dream and realizing it fruitfully. It may well be that your personnel cannot visualize the dream but they will sense it. You may still, consequently, be able to create a general sense of the way you would like it to be.

Be aware that your corporate duties and your responsibilities will be important if you wish to retain your integrity. Your stakeholders have an expectation which must be delivered. There will be three obvious stakeholders to consider – your investors, your consumers and your teams. All your stakeholders will have expectations which will need to be managed. Balancing these three stakeholder-groups will not be without its challenges yet designing objectives which meet their requirements can further bring benefits.

An investor will be expecting a return on his investment. The investor will have committed his resources in return for a promise of a healthy return. Managing unrealistic expectations will be part of your brief as a leader. Understand that people naturally have expectations and sometimes these will be unrealistic. If you allow your investor to retain his unrealistic expectations unchanged you will risk his disappointment. This principle will similarly apply to members of your team and your clients.

Your consumer will expect a level of service which reflects well on his investment. Developing a great relationship with your client will be essential if you are to satisfy his expectations.

> *A leader without vision will be like a letter without a stamp – it will never reach its destination.*

INNOVATION

All men dream: but not equally. Those who dream by night in the dusty recesses of their minds wake in the day to find that it was vanity: but the dreamers of the day are dangerous men, for they may act their dreams with open eyes, to make it possible. This I did.

T. E. Lawrence

You will need to be innovative and adventurous but never reckless while subtly managing any change.

You will need to banish any self-doubt while your change is evolving. There should be no room for doubt or scope for hesitation in your mind. You must drive your business forward as if your reputation depended on it.

You alone will be responsible for the outcome of your plans but you should never indulge in self-blame if the outcome is not exactly what you had expected.

COURAGE

*Courage is resistance to fear, mastery of fear –
not the absence of fear.*

Mark Twain

Courage means that you should be daring rather than confrontational. If you have courage you will be devoid of self-doubt once you are on a mission.

Your courage will be contagious. People will follow you because you will lead courageously. If you have courage in the face of adversity then you will set the tone for your organization and its people.

RESOURCEFULNESS

Seek out that particular mental attribute
which makes you feel most deeply and vitally
alive, along with which comes the inner voice
which says, 'This is the real me,' and when you
have found that attitude, follow it.

William James

You can make everything look easy because you are resourceful.

You must have an abundance of excellent personal resources which you can utilize in order to improve your organization's performance.

The art of modelling will allow you to analyse someone's else's behaviour and then to adopt that behaviour as if it were your own. Your model could, for instance, utilize humour as an effective communication tactic which you could emulate in your own way.

You should continually look for ways of becoming resourceful and maintain your energy-levels. Your colleagues will also spot your resourcefulness once you have developed this facility.

INSPIRATION

> *To inspire is an implant ... to motivate is an*
> *injection ... to manipulate is an infection ...*

> **Doug Firebaugh**

If you want to be inspirational then you must be passionate. Passionate people are committed in heart and mind to act with purpose. Without passion you will have no spark with which to ignite the inspiration of your team. An inspirational leader will have passion which will seem to be embossed in his ethos.

If you are an inspiration to your team you should see the world and its people as exciting and laden with opportunity. Your dialogue will then be filled with passion and direction and it will, consequently, become infectious.

You should be a front-runner in the purposeful pursuit of your vision. You should be driven and focused on the outcome. Your passion will make the impossible possible. Your appetite will create an emotional connection which will evoke an intuitive response. Your fiery passion will fire people up without the need for factual persuasion.

DIFFERENTIATION

I walk slowly, but I never walk backward.

Abraham Lincoln

What differentiates you will define you. Learn to understand what is different about you compared with the rest of the crowd.

Everyone will be unique in some way. Even one individual's energy signature can be very different from another person's aura. One person can come across as full of energy and dynamic while another individual may be calm yet have a commanding presence.

Consider any of the world's extraordinary leaders and identify what differentiates each. These leaders are constructive, engaging and constantly seeking to add value into any and every situation.

Make a list of your differences – perhaps with the help of those close to you – and consider what people have said about you. Now you will really get to the core of who you are and the way in which you are perceived by others.

SIMPLICITY

Knowledge is a process of piling up facts;
wisdom lies in their simplification.

Martin H. Fischer

Simplicity will be a prerequisite of sophistication. A leader who thrives on simplicity will be more agile.

The less complicated your systems and processes are the easier it will be for your organization to adapt to changing circumstances. You will thus be able to manoeuvre your business at short notice when things are simple. If you have fewer moving parts in your vessel this will result in fewer breakdowns.

> *The rotary engine is a clever and complex invention. The simpler diesel engine, however, dominates the commercial transportation industry.*

DIPLOMACY

You can fool all the people some of the time, and some of the people all the time, but you cannot fool all the people all the time.

Abraham Lincoln

Diplomacy should be ingrained in all your communication if you are to make a difference and if you wish to create a legacy.

You must focus on the best possible outcome for your organization and then achieve your purpose diplomatically. If the prevailing circumstances are fixed then you must extract the best results while still maintaining respect for any other party and not allowing hostility to enter into the negotiation.

INCLUSIVITY

A business has to be involving, it has to be fun,
and it has to exercise your creative instincts.

Richard Branson

If you isolate yourself from your personnel you will create an internal culture of separation which may be detrimental to your organization's growth.

If you detach yourself from your organization then you will risk losing control and you will not be aware of any subtle nuances of dissention or cultural change.

If you are reticent then your team will detect your reserve and may adopt an aggressive culture which will upset the delicate balance of power in your organization. You must, therefore, embed an inclusive corporate culture into your organization by setting the scene.

> *One person might be ecstatic with a dish of caviar*
> *while the other feels nauseous at the idea.*

EXEMPLARY CONDUCT

*People do not buy goods and services. They
buy relationships, stories and magic.*

Seth Godin

Your personnel should be made aware that you will perform your role in an exemplary manner and that you will be leading by personal example.

Your personal example will positively influence your followers. You should demonstrate to your personnel the efficiency of the way in which you engage and execute your duties. You must walk the talk with integrity if you want to encourage your team to act similarly. You cannot, for instance, accuse a team-member of unpalatable malpractice if you commit the same fault yourself.

INTEGRITY

*The most important persuasion tool you have
in your entire arsenal is integrity.*

Zig Ziglar

People will value integrity and so you should endeavour to be honest with yourself and with others. You must thus be comfortable with yourself so that you can inspire others to behave in a similar fashion.

A leader who has integrity will live up to his values. Always ensure, consequently, that what you say will be what you do because integrity will be a key leadership strength.

Your leadership strength will be built on a foundation of trust and this conviction will then trickle down throughout your organization. Your moral compass will be evident because of your actions, deeds and communication.

OPENNESS

The truth will out.

William Shakespeare

You must cultivate open and honest relationships. If you are transparent you will never create an air of suspicion. If you want to be believed you should not be guarded.

If you appear to be transparent you will be perceived as genuine and authentic. You should, therefore, behave sincerely and not be fearful of doing so. If you are fearful or uncaring this nature will sooner or later reveal itself. It would be better, therefore, to address these concerns prior to committing yourself to a leadership role. By shifting your perception you can alter your perspective both of yourself or your take on any situation.

Where ambiguity exists people will make up their own narrative. Gossip and rumour will start to become truth. As long as everyone knows what is happening then suspicion will be removed and certainty will provide the security which your personnel require in order to function with confidence.

TRANSPARENCY

> *Perception is strong and sight weak. In strategy*
> *it is important to see distant things as if they*
> *were close and to take a distanced view of close*
> *things.*

Miyamoto Musashi

Your actions and your demeanour must be transparent because this tactic will be critical to the success of your enterprise.

Your personnel must form a relationship with you which will be based on trust. You must, therefore, fulfil your team's expectation of trust in you which you can genuinely deliver. If you communicate honestly in words and deeds you will automatically foster healthy relationships which will be built on a foundation of transparency.

You will need to address your emotive life in order to attain transparency so that your mindset and your accompanying attitude will be congruent with your integrity. You can only achieve transparency when you are self-congruent and self-assured.

If you find yourself being hypocritical or lacking conviction it may be indicative of your lack of self-esteem and self-worth. If you struggle with being challenged by someone who has opposing views then you may tend to want to please your opponent rather than being genuine.

CO-OPERATION

All our knowledge has its origin in our perceptions.

Leonardo Da Vinci

A great leader will know that he cannot do it on his own.

Develop the necessary skills in order to engage with people at all levels, have a wide and varied social and business network and maintain healthy relationships. You will then come across as a caring and compassionate individual although you will be constantly keeping an eye on the big picture.

Step into another person's shoes, even if only momentarily, in order to understand him better and appreciate what he might be feeling so that you can help him to overcome any issues. You will thus show that you care and your consideration will be reciprocated. When you combine your compassion with a high degree of emotional intelligence you will become a most memorable leader.

You will, of course, need to recognize and to manage your own feelings which will, in turn, affect your team's emotive reactions. Simply endeavour to understand each of your team-members and then find the most appropriate way to help each one. Do not, however, exhaust yourself by endeavouring to please everyone and by attempting to achieve everything at once.

TRUST

*Faith is an oasis in the heart which will never
be reached by the caravan of thinking.*

Kahlil Gibran

Your personnel will be astute enough to know whether you reliably mean what you say through your actions. Your team, therefore, should be guided by a healthy compass as your duty of care in order to achieve excellent results.

Sometimes you must simply ask for what you want particularly when fast action and urgency are dictated. Immediacy is what will be needed in this situation but never in a state of panic.

Your team will also be able to detect whether you are caring and compassionate. If you have faith in your personnel you will empower your team-members in order to carry out their work in a manner which will be effective. If you formulate an objective then simply trust that your personnel will achieve it without too much interference and micro-managing from you.

Having faith in your organization's managers can be evident in a leader who avoids micro-managing. You should formulate the objective and then allow those responsible for carrying it out to do it in their own way.

RESPECTFULNESS

The secret of leadership is simple: Do what you believe in. Paint a picture of the future. Go there. People will follow.

Seth Godin

If you have a healthy respect for everyone you will empower your personnel.

An appreciation of what makes different people feel respected will be an important leadership skill for you to develop. Consider how you personally might feel when you are shown respect and how you feel when you are treated disrespectfully.

You will need to develop the art of listening to others in order to be influential even if you have no-one reporting directly to you. Never underestimate the effect you may have on others because you will inevitably cause a ripple in the pond somewhere.

GRATITUDE

*All that is necessary for the triumph of evil is
that good men do nothing.*

Edmund Burke

Your personnel should feel valued for their efforts and their contribution to your goals.

When you show your appreciation to others you will add to your own leadership value. An act of appreciation and gratitude delivered with humility and sincerity will considerably help to develop strong and fruitful relationships with your personnel. If you can develop a culture of kindness you will be forming a well-bonded team with one common purpose.

You should always actively listen with interest and curiosity to what your team-member will be saying. You will, by this means, lift your personnel higher by making each one feel that he is making a significant contribution. If you are self-assured you will share the credit with all involved in the team-effort.

You should endeavour to create a working environment in which mutual respect, gratitude and fun are abundant and continually present. This environment will then generate and celebrate success for your organization and negativity will be banished.

KEY PERSONAL QUALITIES

I would rather try to persuade a man to go along, because once I have persuaded him, he will stick. If I scare him, he will stay just as long as he is scared, and then he is gone.

Dwight D. Eisenhower

LEADERSHIP ASSETS

You should endeavour to develop yourself as an individual who will display those personal qualities which will propel you to the top.

The development of your personal qualities will entail some self-searching on your part but your task will not be erroneous, thankless or devoid of reward.

SELF-DISCIPLINE

Self-discipline will be the first step towards mindful self-mastery. The ability to control yourself will be necessary if you are to control your destiny. You can harness self-discipline by developing constructive wilfulness and delayed gratification. If you possess self-discipline you will be able to focus on your objective and not compromise your goal by being distracted by immediate gains.

Firstly you will need to control your own train of thought. This will be a little like pressing the pause button of a video – you can bring everything to a standstill. Once you can feel calm you will be able to reflect on a particular situation and you can then look carefully and dispassionately at your options in order to find a better solution.

SELF-AWARENESS

Self-awareness will give you greater confidence in your abilities and will allow you to identify those elements which you can change. In becoming more self-aware you will also become more aware of others.

Simplicity of style will be the hallmark of a successful leader. You will need to develop skills which will make you fully aware of yourself and conscious of your environment. You should similarly understand your team-members in order to generate your collective success.

When you possess focused self-awareness you will be able to concentrate on the task in hand while still retaining an awareness of the big picture. You can, for instance, read a book while still being aware of everything peripheral around you but without distraction.

You should endeavour to focus on what you can change about yourself by becoming more self-aware. If you are attentive to your own tone of voice and you can consider your words carefully you will effect great change in the way in which you are received by others.

You should also become aware of your personal appearance and your body language. This will be something which you can change. It may be worth spending time on designing your appearance so that it will give the appropriate impression. You will also need to be aware of your style, vitality, mindset and the attitude which you portray. These qualities will indicate the level of care and support which you can offer your personnel.

If you have a particular skill for inspiring individuals and groups then become aware of this faculty in order to develop excellence. If you realize that you possess the ability to influence others then you can utilize this gift appropriately.

You must also acknowledge any of your shortcomings which cannot be altered. Once you know what your unalterable limitations are then you will be in a position to find an appropriate solution. You may, for instance, need to find people who can help support you. You can, in this way, build a network of peers who can add value to your mission without attempting to over-stretch yourself.

> *An orchestral conductor will not be paying attention to just one instrument. The conductor's objective will be to ensure that everyone will be playing in harmony. It will be up to the conductor to direct the orchestra as a whole and not to be overly distracted by an individual who may need to be corrected.*
>
> *Each section of the orchestra will have its own leader and it will be up to the conductor to convey any necessary instructions to the lead-player without losing focus himself.*

SELF-CONVICTION

You must ensure that your self-conviction and your self-belief are steadfast in order to be able to motivate your team. Your own self-belief will transmit itself to your team-members who may then follow your exemplary lead.

When you possess a strong self-belief you will indirectly imply a commitment to your duty because of your self-conviction which, in turn, will be conveyed to your team. Often your team-members will seek to emulate your ideals. When your purpose is clear those who follow you will be equally enthused by your overall commitment.

If you can give your team an opportunity to embrace your self-belief you will become the kingpin which will drive your organization forward. You and your team can thus become a formidable force which will be bound together by a common belief about your mission. Your self-conviction, therefore, will cultivate your team's certainty and be a strong motivating force. It might be better to explore fearlessly than to attack at the first sign of a challenge.

Do not attempt to conceal your lack of conviction behind a mask of fear-based arrogance and grandiosity in the hope that your team will not notice. Any lack of self-conviction may be evident when you begin to attack others and will further amplify your own fear. Defending a position vigorously can also be evidence of your lack of self-assuredness.

> *A violin soloist might challenge the conductor about the interpretation of a particular piece of music and the way in which it should to be timed and played. The conductor might consider the player's opinion and choose to reconsider or not. He would be unwise to dismiss or challenge the violinist.*

SELF-RELIANCE

You must believe that you have a value which will allow you to make a major contribution to your enterprise. You must, consequently, have unwavering faith in your own ability to bring your vision to fruition.

A belief in your ability to learn and to change will be as vital as your ability to manage your own expectations and those of others carefully.

Self-reliance will mean that you will have faith in your mind's ability to create the pathways towards your vision. If you dispel any personal doubts then your team will be clambering to accompany you on your journey.

If you harbour a fear of success, however, this uncertainty will be born from a lack of your self-worth and this notion will rob you of your potential.

AUTHENTICITY

You should strive to be authentic and genuine because most people will be able to differentiate between the genuine and the disingenuous.

If you are disingenuous you may be easily fooled by disingenuous praise from others. You will relinquish your personal power if your intention will be to receive approval or to seek to impress others. If your vision is to create something great then you will need to avoid the trap of seeking personal approval.

CHARISMA

Your leadership presence will empower your team to rise to any challenge by adopting a positive approach. Your charisma will radiate and maintain your presence. Your presence will distinguish you from the rest of the pack.

You should develop a presence which others can instantly recognize so that you will stand out in the crowd and you will get noticed. There should be something indefinable about you which attracts others. You should, for instance, be at ease with yourself and you must maintain a presence which subtly permeates the minds of those with whom you interact.

Your presence should convey to others a deeper understanding of your environment and the world about you. You can, in this way, remain steadfast even in the event of turmoil without appearing arrogant, becoming threatening or feeling insecure. You may even feel humble and cherish every opportunity of helping others.

> *An accomplished orchestral conductor will convey his message to the orchestra who will follow his direction implicitly. The conductor will be able to conduct the orchestra in such a way that he allows for few errors while permitting the individual musicians to use their skills and personality in order to deliver their best performance.*

ENCHANTMENT

Enchantment is the ability to help people feel good about themselves to the point where they want to be involved in making your vision a reality. Enchantment will be the key to the hearts and minds of your personnel.

You should accept every individual whom you meet unconditionally. You ought to make every person you meet feel good about himself so that he will follow you.

Enchantment can be very alluring when it is sincere and especially when it is delivered with a degree of humour and playfulness.

PERCEPTUAL AGILITY

You will not be able to achieve what you cannot perceive. You will perceive those things which command your attention.

If you assume that an individual will react emotively in given circumstances then you can begin to understand that it should be your personnel's beliefs which you will need to influence. You must, therefore, be flexible so that you can adjust your tactics in ever-changing circumstances.

Your thinking skills will develop perceptual agility. You can begin this process by observing the way in which others adapt to any new challenge.

OPEN-MINDEDNESS

An open-minded leader will be approachable. There are few successful leaders who have a closed and fixed view.

If you decide without seeking and understanding the views of other people you will risk failure. If you obtain a number of different views you will be able to explore several perspectives which may, in fact, yield far better results than your single-track decision.

If you are open to new ideas you can have no fear of allowing someone else to influence you but instead you will actually encourage others to contribute to your vision fully.

POSITIVE THINKING

Your internal dialogue must be constructive and focused positively. When your self-talk is destructive you will be harming yourself.

You cannot afford to have a voice in your head which spreads fear and doubt. This voice must be silenced and replaced with a voice of support which encourages a let's-do-this attitude.

You will hence need to challenge any states of self-doubt without endlessly analysing the past so that you can design the future. Do not, therefore, keep doing what you have always done because you will always get the same negative result. If you are, in any way, uncertain then seek the opinion of an expert in order to generate some alternative ideas which you may not have previously considered.

MENTAL FACULTIES

Perception is such an important function of the mind yet so little time is normally invested in understanding its importance. Logic still rules in the realms of intelligence and little value is given to perceptual agility.

Edward de Bono

DEVELOP YOURSELF

You should appreciate the importance of self-development as an individual in order to excel in your leadership role. Your self-development will consist of professional self-development and personal self-development.

When you develop professionally you will need to enhance your education and skill-set to the best of your ability in order to grow with your team. You should also acquire effective social skills so that you can communicate effectively with your team and your stakeholders.

When you develop personally you will be at peace with yourself. You should be comfortable with who you are and self-congruent in all you undertake while, at the same time, continually seeking self-improvement so that you can inspire others. Your ideal will be to unashamedly love what you do.

You must, of course, banish any fears or trepidation about your action so that you will not be inhibited in any way. Without personal fear you will be able to inspire your team and challenge your own ideas.

> *A gardener may enjoy tending to a rosebush even though there are no flowers for him to enjoy. The gardener's pleasure will be derived from tending to the plant, by taking care in pruning and feeding the plant. His pleasure in gardening activity will be apparent even when the roses do not bloom.*

CREATIVE THINKING

Your mind will enjoy the creative challenge of problem-solving. You should, therefore, not employ your thinking activity only when a crisis occurs.

There are three basic thinking styles which will be essential for you in order to function efficiently and effectively.

Constructive thinking

Your constructive thinking ability will assist you when evaluating your objectives and when assessing your own judgement.

Critical thinking

Your critical thinking ability will allow you to evaluate a situation, a product or a service.

Creative thinking

Your creative thinking ability will permit you to embrace a fast-changing environment and to evolve your organization.

The dreamer will be the creative thinker, the realist will be the constructive thinker and the critical thinker will be the critic.

A dreamer will not be able to make a dream become a reality without the realist to deal with the practical steps of getting things done. The realist and the critic will never be able to envisage a great goal without the vision of the dreamer. If you enhance your constructive, critical and creative thinking, therefore, you will ensure your own all-round success. If you favour one style at the expense of another you may be limiting yourself considerable.

When you approach any demanding situation you should select an appropriate thinking style. You will be able to apply the appropriate thinking style by perceiving the value in any situation and then make adjustments accordingly.

> *Walt Disney built a massive empire that has endured and grown over the decades. In modelling Walt Disney's thinking styles, it was discovered that he had an uncanny ability to switch from one thinking style to another.*
>
> *If someone approached him with an idea for creating something amazing he might step into the role of the critic and challenge the dreamer by pointing out the difficulties and challenges and risks faced by such a huge project.*

MENTAL ATTITUDES

You should learn how to understand the attitude and approach which you would normally adopt when interacting with others.

Your mindset will have a predetermined view which will govern your approach to others and the outcome of your negotiations. Your mental attitude will determine whether you are, for example, friendly, aggressive or kind.

You could begin to alter your mindset by deciding whether your attitude will benefit or will hinder a given situation. You might also consider whether you have the capacity to adapt or to adopt your attitude in order to encourage co-operation and respect from others.

> *Disney's vision was to make people happy. If you judge by results then children's faces will attest to the fact that Disney accomplished his mission.*

MENTAL STATES

You should learn how to managing your emotive and mental states and your connection with the environment.

You must learn to become aware of your baseline state and your default reaction to events. When you understand your natural baseline reaction you will be able to determine whether this default state will help you or will hinder you.

Your ideal state of mind should keep you clear, focused and connected with your task and oblivious of anything else because you will be totally immersed and tuned into yourself.

You should always avoid being in a non-resourceful state which could generate overwhelm, exhaustion and fear. Once you gain this self-understanding you will be able to switch from one state to another automatically. Do not, therefore, restrict yourself to a limited number of mental and emotive states because you will be handicapped by your limitations. If you only know how to be an aggressor or a victim then this will be your only response.

CONCEPTUAL THINKING

A concept is a broad vista rather than a specific idea. If you can encourage your team to adopt conceptual thinking you will generate new ideas with high value and make important discoveries.

It will be part of your remit to challenge any entrenched concepts which your team-members may have formed and could have accepted as gospel. Historical continuity will be the enemy of evolution.

You must be alert to every opportunity for innovation. You must, therefore, encourage your team to look for opportunities for improvements and cost-saving. You might also consider rewarding your personnel with an incentive if someone makes a significant contribution to your organization's evolution.

> *If a man retains the concept that peanut butter is simply a spread then he cannot evolve his limited thinking. If he were to consider peanut butter as a filling then he could progress to creating a cupcake filled with peanut butter. This man has now created an exciting new recipe idea.*

THINKING HATS

The Six Thinking Hats technique is one of the most powerful tools which will empower you to think clearly, efficiently, effectively and creatively by adopting parallel thinking.

You should consider every type of thinking style prior to making any decision when using parallel thinking. You should focus on the whole picture by thinking in six different ways about each component of your problem in order to extract its value before moving your attention on to the next factor. If you don a specific coloured hat for a particular thinking style you will see your difficulty from many perspectives and each viewpoint will become memorable.

The blue hat

The blue hat will manage your thinking process from the big picture perspective. The blue hat will outline what you are thinking about and will lay out your guidelines.

The white hat

The white hat will identify known and unknown information.

The black hat

The black hat will tell you when you might need to be cautious, what the possible dangers might be in action or inaction and will assess your level of risk.

The red hat

The red hat will handle your feelings, hunches and intuition without the need to justify or to substantiate your decision-making.

The yellow hat

The yellow hat will extract the benefits of action and will assess the value of taking action.

The green hat

The green hat will focus on your alternatives and will consider any alternative approaches.

You ought to invest time in learning and applying thinking skills in your everyday life, hone your thinking clarity and ensure that your team-members will all be on the same page. You will become far more confident in your decision-making and you could save hours of procrastination by having more constructive meetings with your team by following the formula of the Six Thinking Hats model.

> *A company in Australia frequently gives its personnel a day to work from home so that each employee can think about every aspect of the organization and suggest ways of making improvements and this policy has reaped numerous benefits.*

SELF-BELIEF

Have no fear of perfection.
You'll never reach it.

Salvador Dali

SELF-EMPOWERMENT

Your self-belief will generate your ability to start your organization on a journey and to believe it every step of the way. You must be able to ponder your options and possibilities and to explore alternatives along the way without allowing self-doubt to creep into the equation.

You must have a sound belief in yourself as a leader and your vision and be assured that you possess the necessary skills in order to achieve your objectives.

BELIEF RESTRUCTURING

If you harbour any limiting self-belief you will need to establish communication with your reasoning and you should specifically explore your negative beliefs. If you can freely extract your negative core beliefs from within your mind you will then be able to perceive the underlying pattern which will influence your behaviour.

A belief is an assumption which you will directly or indirectly form from the foundation of your experience. Once a belief has been established in your mind you will react automatically as a consequence.

You should endeavour to construct a complete picture of your belief system in order to understand your behaviour, your motivation, your perspective, your attitudes and your perception. At your core will be a well-constructed bedrock of experiences which will be recorded in your mind because of past events. Your mind will have felt an emotion and will have applied some reasoning to a given situation at the time when your beliefs were originally formed.

SELF-ORGANIZING BELIEFS

Your beliefs will form a self-organizing belief structure within your mind. Every new belief you adopt will be built into your existing belief structure and the whole structure will then reorganize accordingly.

Your collective set of beliefs will form the basis of your future perception, expectations, attitudes, convictions, assumptions and presupposition about forthcoming events. Your belief system will become the premise from which your mind will operate according to the structure which has been created.

Your beliefs will dictate your value-judgements and will influence your perception of events. If your beliefs were created by an untoward event in your life whatever belief you form at the time will apply unfailingly in every similar situation and can be paralyzing for you.

> *A client in his mid-thirties worked in the financial services sector as a senior manager. This client had rejected a number of opportunities for promotion to director-level because he felt that he could not fulfil the function of a director even though he knew he was still at his peak.*
>
> *It transpired, of course, that the client had foregone the benefits of promotion previously in order to avoid experiencing terror. Apparently the client believed that he would be laughed at and mimicked if he stood up in order to speak in front of others.*

BELIEF COMPONENTS

Your perception, your emotions and your beliefs will be interwoven. You will not be able to perceive anything which your mind cannot recognize as meaningful.

Your mind will perceive meaning before you can make any decisions and you will classify incoming information according to your belief structure. If, for instance, you have previously reacted to a situation with fear then your perception will be coloured by this untoward experience when you later encounter a similar incident.

Your beliefs, your perception and your attitudes will be transparent to those around you. Your emotive reactions, therefore, could overwhelm you quite unexpectedly in certain circumstances and you will then be unable to counteract your feelings. When you perceive fear, whether real or imagined, which could affect you adversely in times of crisis you will need to take immediate action in order to banish your fear – even if you need to seek professional help.

> *A ship's captain must set a direction which he will have plotted with his expert navigators. The captain's belief in the direction which he has elected to take will be essential if the ship is to arrive at its destination safely and on time.*

ENHANCING POSITIVE BELIEFS

The effect which your beliefs can have on the way in which you perceive and experience life can be mapped out in such a way that the result will give you the power to choose which beliefs are worth keeping and which require changing or eliminating.

If you can banish your limiting beliefs you will better yourself and you can change your life-experience. You should, therefore, endeavour to develop a positive set of beliefs in order to empower yourself so that you can take appropriate action, improve your personal performance and realize your full potential. A steadfast belief in your own ability, for instance, will be a self-belief which will underpin your leadership mission.

Your positive attitude and self-belief will enhance the optimism of your team and will encourage each individual team-member to adopt a similar attitude. Your leadership attitudes of humility, compassion and understanding, for instance, will be a highly desirable commodity.

RESOLVING NEGATIVE BELIEFS

You should take responsibility for discovering the origin of all your negative beliefs with a view to banishing negativity and self-doubt. Your beliefs will either motivate you and your team or could dilute your mission statement and demoralize you.

If you emanate any lack of sound self-conviction, however, you will, almost certainly, generate discord or suspicion which will detrimentally affect your organization, its people and its consumers. You will create a negative aura around yourself and your team will detect it and then under-perform, lack commitment or only feign engagement.

You will need to address your underlying negative belief by identifying your action and then asking yourself what might be holding you back before the situation crumbles irretrievably. If you can eliminate your negative beliefs you will obtain a clearer view of your corporate objectives because you will be able to view your purpose objectively. You cannot afford to be uncertain in your actions, ambiguous when giving instructions or doubt your decision-making ability.

Any lack of self-belief will mean that you may experience difficulty in decision-making and you will probably make rash, brash or hazardous decisions. If you believe that you will fail then you may stumble and bumble along because of your underlying lack of self-belief. If you feel at all threatened, for instance, by your team then your negative self-belief may need to be examined. If you have an inherent self-blame tendency then you may look over your shoulder and see your own catalogue of errors.

LEADERSHIP ROADMAP

Plans are nothing; planning is everything.

Dwight D. Eisenhower

REALIZING VISION

Your vision can be brought to fruition by conveying the principles of your dream, formulating your objectives and then communicating your ideas effectively to your team.

If your instructions to your team about your vision are vague or unclear, or you fail to communicate your objective completely, then the result could be confusion and possibly disaster.

If you can appreciate the place you want to reach you can then formulate your objective, construct your plan of action accurately and keep your goal in sight at all times and in all weathers.

When you formulate your objectives you should consider what you want as your desired outcome in order to ensure that the result of your planning and action will be the one which you desire. A well-planned objective with a positive outcome, therefore, will warrant adequate consideration from you in order to guarantee its success.

Your objectives must have your broad vision embedded in every decision taken along the way towards attaining your goal. Your vision must, consequently, be threaded through the culture of your organization.

When bringing your vision and your objective to fruition you will need take aim at your known goal and you should have a purpose in your undertaking.

> *A ship's captain will convey the principles of his vision to the navigator. The co-ordinates of the captain's mission will be entered into the navigational computer system as his objectives.*
>
> *The path towards realizing these objectives will finally be communicated to the crew who will abide by their instructions. The components of the captain's vision will be accomplished step by step and will result in a successful voyage.*

FORMULATING OBJECTIVES

Your objectives should provide a range of benefits and an impetus which will result in your organization's continued growth.

Some of your objectives may seek a short-term benefit while others may look at the medium-term or the long-term.

Your objectives may also vary in terms of value. Some of your objectives may be critical while others may be merely exploratory.

Clearly specified objectives will be vital so that all every team-member will be able to comprehend precisely what he must implement. If your goal-specification is confusing or is ambiguous then you will be at the mercy of your team's interpretation of your ideas.

Your objectives must also be sufficiently well analysed before any action can be taken so that you can assess the risk-reward equation. The tendency – particularly when times are tough – may be for you to be reactive rather than proactive. When a crisis occurs, therefore, you may be inclined to take risks because of your desperation.

Your objectives must also be time-bound when action is taken. If your team fails to act quickly then by the time your destination is actually reached it may well be too late.

If your objectives need to change when circumstances dictate you should ensure that you can overcome any resistance to change by outlining the benefit of such change in order to allow your team to work towards attaining any new goals.

> *A farmer's produce may be ready to be picked, packed and shipped to the wholesalers. Any delay in taking the appropriate action may mean that the farmer's produce will perish.*

FORMULATING PLANS

Once your objectives have been set you will need to formulate an action plan in order to ensure that your mission will be accomplished successfully. If your plans are flawed or even non-existent your objective will not come to fruition.

Your plans should be more than just a description of the actions which you propose to take but should become a means of measuring progress and making fine adjustments when necessary.

Your team must fully digest your action plan which can act as a reference-point. Your plans should, therefore, be in keeping with your organization's ideology and values and should become an anchor on which your team can depend.

Your organization's core values and focus should be incorporated in your action plans. Your plans should specify, for instance, whether your organization is concerned with producing mass products for the consumer at low prices or yielding a high return for your shareholders.

It will be important for you to implement your plan only after due consideration has been given to all aspects of its implementation. Time invested in exploring alternatives and possibilities when formulating your plans will enrich your choices.

Your plans should also include a degree of flexibility so that you can change course if circumstances alter and your target may be constantly shifting. If you cannot maintain your objective then your plans will need to be flexible enough to accommodate this change of tactic. If resources, for instance, are unavailable or you cannot justify expenditure then your plans will need to be flexible enough to cope with this circumstantial change.

> *If a man decides to go to a distant town it would be useful for him to plan his route. He could lay out a map and look at where he needs to reach and then evaluate the different choices available to him. The man might want to stop at a certain point in order to recharge or look at something in particular. The man might stop and visit a friend or he might want to deliver a parcel.*

REVIEWING PROGRESS

You will need to allocate time for reflection about your organization's progress and its future. You must evaluate your organization's requirements, find solutions to any outstanding issues and consider your direction.

You will frequently need to involve your team in any review process. A team review can assist you to analyse your objectives and thus ensure that each team-member is on track. A review meeting can also unify your team as each team-member will then work collectively towards your goal.

It may be helpful for you to provoke your team into solving a hypothetical problem in order to jockey your personnel into finding a solution to an existing difficulty.

If you can challenge each stage of your progress you will be able to visualize the way in which each progressive phase might be approached differently. Encouraging your team to be opportunist will be another important part of your organizational tactic. Your team, therefore, should learn to think critically, be constantly vigilant for new opportunities to improve and develop foresight.

> *A ship's captain may well hold an emergency drill in order to evacuate the passengers and crew. Not because there is a fire on board but, when the drill is done repeatedly, it will become second nature to the participants. Should a fire break out then the crew will know instinctively what action to take in order to safeguard the ship, its passengers and its cargo.*

REVIEWING STRUCTURE

You may find that a review of your organizational structure could lead you to decide that a deconstruction and reconfiguration will be required. The inherent structure of your organization may be well established and generally accepted as the norm by all your personnel but this situation may, however, not be ideal.

You could consider the way in which your organization would be structured if you were starting from scratch as a means of transforming your structure. Often this mental exercise will highlight the way in which you will need to redesign your organizational structure and to specify where changes should be implemented.

You might also consider whether an existing conventional pyramidal structure or a layer structure is the most suitable for your organization or whether a streamlined approach might be more appropriate. Sometimes a given structure will have a limited life – especially if your organization is growing rapidly.

> *Recently there was a shift in space-rocket technology with the launch of Japan's Epsilon rocket at the cost of £23 million. Apparently it can be launched with a ground crew of only 15 people and at about one tenth of what it would cost at NASA. Technological developments have made this possible.*
>
> *Other space agencies will now need to adapt in order to compete.*

FORMULATING STRATEGY

Without a strategy you will generate chaos because your personnel will be left to their own devices. A well-designed strategy will bring your vision into reality and your tactics will then be the means of achieving your vision.

You may need to devise a global and evolutionary strategy for your organization together with a number of specific strategies for several different purposes.

Your strategy should be viewed as the broad approach to conducting your organization's business. Your strategy will be concerned, therefore, with whether your enterprise exists to provide a service, to offer the lowest-price product on the market or to supply the greatest range of products.

Your broad-brush strategy must be carefully considered so that your fee-paying customers will easily be able to grasp the intention of your enterprise. Once you have designed your overall corporate strategy then you can employ specific and detailed tactics in order to achieve your aim. Each subordinate team-leader will need to appreciate your broad strategy so that he can then design any mechanical tactics for your enterprise's personnel.

Your strategy will usually deal with the long-term approach for the organization and will guide your actions and your decision-making processes accordingly. Your strategy, of course, must be flexible enough to cater for any unforeseen eventuality in practice.

> *A footballer takes aim towards the net between the posts in order to score a goal. The footballer's objective will be to win the game. If the footballer's aims and goal-scoring are sufficient his team may reach the top of the league.*

LEADERSHIP TACTICS

Leadership and learning are indispensable to each other.

J F Kennedy

INVOLVING TEAMS

You should secure your team's interest in your vision and then ensure that your quest has been understood, accepted and supported by every team-member without compromise.

Sometimes your objectives will need to be formulated with your team's full knowledge and input. You could, for instance, exploit your team's skills and you might elicit views by exploring viable options. This tack can give you an opportunity to consider a number of different viewpoints even though the final decision will be your own.

A group-consensus may also allow your team to become aware of each team-member's contribution and requirements. You will also be affording your team an opportunity for taking your organization forward.

This group-decision ploy will also provide your team with an opportunity to understand your objective fully. Your team-members will not necessarily comprehend your vision without some form of personal involvement and constructive input.

You may need to weigh up the merits of team inclusivity when formulating your objectives and setting your targets. If your team is overly involved in decision-making, for instance, this situation may engender power-play by one of your influential team-members.

A fragmented team which cannot operate as one entity could be catastrophic. You can only fire up your team-members when unity exists and each team-member will be wholeheartedly involved in generating the success of your objective. Your alternative will be to carry the load on your own back and perhaps be forced to negotiate with an obstinate team-member.

You should aim to keep your team focused and constantly aware of progress. If your team is clearly focused on the objectives to be attained then its members will become united in their collective purpose.

The idea that a team-member will fail to support, assist, encourage and promote your objective should be treated by you with zero-tolerance. If you cannot lead your team to success then this situation will be the undoing of your organization.

You should also make time for creative and lateral thinking with your team so that new ideas can be examined and existing processes and procedures can be simplified when necessary.

> *The captain of a ship asks three members of his crew where to fish. One of the crew-members will point east, one south and the other west. If the captain and his crew-members reach a compromise by heading north then who will be satisfied in this equation?*

If the crew of a ship fails to unite then the objective of reaching the ship's destination will be seriously be hampered.

DELIVERING VALUE

Behind every action there must be a number of values which can deliver benefits for you.

A project should contain sufficient value for your team so that each team-member can become motivated. Where insufficient value exists in a project your team will not fully engage with your plans or will only feign an interest. You should, therefore, assess your objectives in terms of differing values. You might also need to appreciate who the benefactors will be when your objective has been reached.

You could pose a number of questions which will help you to discover the value contained within your objectives:

Will your objective be of benefit to the operator?

Could benefit be concerned with simplifying a process or a lengthy procedure?

Could an operator be rendered more efficient?

Might an operator be more able to enjoy the process because of the removal of contention from a situation?

Will your objective be to deliver better value to the consumer?

Will your aim be to improve a service, a quality or a design?

Will your purpose be a drive to reduce the cost or to increase the value to the consumer?

Will your objective be designed for your organization's growth?

Will you be endeavouring to increase profitability?

Will you need to look at the bottom line so that your stakeholder's reward will be increased?

Will your objective expect your team to take your organization to a new place?

Will your objective be to improve operations in order to facilitate the introduction of a new service?

Should a new product or a new service be designed, created and taken to market?

When your objective embraces value for your operators, consumers and stakeholders then these parties will buy into your vision and your team will be propelled towards reaching your goal.

You should also formulate stringent performance targets in order to show where your objectives are being met. You must consistently check your personnel's action in order to ensure that your team will be achieving your objectives.

You may, of course, continually need to re-evaluate your project by assessing the various completion stages. The evaluation of your project may also mean that you will never reach a final goal because the ground will keep shifting and you may be required to formulate additional goals along the way.

If you wish to get your organization into a new market, for example, you may find that, once there, you will need to formulate a new objective. It could be that your new objective will be to dominate a particular area of the market which you have penetrated.

> *A trawler may be launched into the sea in order to find fish. The trawler-owner's business will survive by finding fertile fishing grounds in which to trawl and then take its catch to market.*
>
> *The trawler will not go fishing a hundred times and then stop. The trawler's business objective will be to successfully catch fish for as long as its work will be profitable.*

VALUING SIMPLICITY

Confusion can be a recipe for chaos and disorder for your organization and so you should learn to value simplicity. If your objectives or your instructions to your team are complex then you could risk the misinterpretation of your requirements.

Your objectives should be kept as simple as possible without compromising your intended outcome. It may take some time for you to acquire the art of effectively formulating a simple solution to any project difficulties. If you can put a high value on simplicity, particularly in the early planning and design stages of any project, you will be better able to communicate your ideas to your team.

Often it will be better for you to dismantle a procedure rather than to continue to expect your team to cope with complexity. You should not permit your team to cling to a complex procedure which could easily be simplified purely because your team-members are wary of change. Do not think that because a system in your organization is complex it will have more appeal and market-value than a simple process.

You must be able to distinguish between simplicity and complexity in order to be able to respond appropriately to demands. A complex system will require precision from experts who are able to calculate finite terms, manipulate algorithms and perform complex operations. You may need to have a clear overview of a complex system but you will not necessarily need to bother with the minutia.

> *A course participant was asked to identify a process in his organization and to simplify it. This course participant worked in a hotel and described an elaborate towel wrapping and transportation process.*
>
> *By simplifying the towel wrapping process before transporting the towels to the hotel rooms the organization saved in excess of £300,000.00 as well as reducing time-wastage as an intangible cost.*

CULTIVATING ZERO-TOLERANCE

Professional life will not be about who you are but it will be more concerned with what you are doing, how you are doing it and why you do it.

The health of an organization will depend on its performance management systems. Progress measurement will be essential in order to keep on track and to understand where attention may need to be focused in the event of an unwanted issue developing.

Having a robust system in place in order to deal stringently with staff performance at all levels of your organization will be crucial in developing a positive culture. Poor performance and an unpleasant attitude should be dealt with immediately before such conditions begin to infect the rest of the team or your organization. When this situation is not dealt with it could cultivate a toxic culture which, like a petri dish, continues to grow its spores.

It will be wise to let it be known that there is an expectation that all personnel and, indeed, those who make any decisions will be expected to show evidence of their decisions and their decision-making process.

The environment carries the organization's culture. Changing a corporate culture will be like redirecting a river. The larger the organization the harder it will be to effect a change. The good news will be that it is only hard – not impossible – and that those who succeed in this depth of transformation will be truly outstanding.

The key to change will be to make a full assessment of the environment, break down the detail so that you can see the structure and determine its weakest point. Then devise and implement a plan in order to sever that weakest link.

IMPLEMENTING CHANGE

Change will be an essential component of business expansion and your function will be to become the architect for your enterprise's transformation.

You will need to appreciate that when seeking change in your organization you will need to cultivate the environment which can facilitate radical transformation.

You must also be alert to stagnation when your personnel fail to evolve and they have settled into a comfort-zone. Historical continuity can become normality for your organization because it contains the gift of stability for your personnel. You must, however, be dynamic and open to organizational change in order to survive.

The greatest hurdle which you may have to overcome when you are implementing change will usually be employee-resistance in addition to insufficient sponsorship and any unrealistic expectations of others.

Human nature will generally be disinclined to change particularly when the current situation is stable. Most people will shy away from instability at any cost.

You may, therefore, need to present change to your personnel as beneficial and unavoidable. If you can exhibit effective independence of thought, individuality and efficiency in action you will successfully materialize your visionary change.

If you need to cause a shift you may want to create a crisis by design in order to expose weakness with your team. If the budget for your department were to be cut by half or you needed to pick a time to switch two managers for a month you would need to handle this change very delicately. You may well find that this situation will result in an opportunity for the innovators in your team to come up with some extraordinary solutions.

Your organization will, of course, require time to evolve just as DNA will mutate over time. Evolution is not an overnight process but it should not move at a snail's pace. What can happen overnight can be revolutionary although its outcome may be unpredictable. A revolution can produce healthy results or it can generate chaos. It will then take time for the situation to stabilize before the outcome can be evaluated.

You must therefore, carefully consider what changes you will need to implement in order to fulfil the needs of your organization in the long term.

You must also be able to accurately evaluate your own results. You may need, consequently, to assess whether the change you have implemented is working efficiently and whether its introduction has achieved your aim. You might need to challenge your own assumptions, prejudices and perspectives and then employ a fresh tactic and discard the dross before your organization can evolve successfully. You should, in essence, evolve yourself in order to evolve your organization.

> *A gardener will take the time to prepare the land for planting. A builder will prepare the site for development. A teacher must prepare his lesson.*
>
> *Preparation minimizes the risk of failure and maximizes the opportunity for success. A seed will need sunshine, rain, wind, fertile soil and air in order to make it possible for that seed to grow.*

EMBRACING EVOLUTION

If you keep still for any length of time your organization will atrophy. The launching of a new venture and the development of a new concept will be part of the evolution of your organization.

If your organization fails to adapt to the modern world you may be faced with serious consequences. If you explore and challenge your boundaries you will be able to seek new products and services which will lead to success. If you simply focus on protecting your market-share, rather than conquering new territory, you may be treading on dangerous turf.

Corporate change will occur because of new procedures, fluctuating costs and technological advancement, for instance, and all will demand a response from you. The effects of inspiration are not to be underestimated. Once inspiration takes root it is virtually self-propagating. It will outperform most other types of drivers.

ADOPTING CHALLENGE TACTICS

By critically evaluating your ideas and your personnel you will be ensuring that dynamic change can occur by challenging all elements of our enterprise.

If you shy away from challenging an individual team-member you may be missing an important growth-opportunity. Your insight into the mindset and the perspective of your workforce will enlighten you enormously and will keep your finger on the pulse. A formal discourse, for instance, with a team-member which will challenge his mental faculties may reap many rewards for your organization.

A challenge tactic in which your team-member strives for overall improvement and efficiency will be rewarded appropriately. You should, encourage critical thinking among your team-members in order to identify inefficiencies rather than taking a confrontational approach in order to find a workable solution to any problem which has been highlighted.

Critical thinking should be encouraged but do not fall into the trap of over-interfering with your team's work and its problem-solving methodology. Your function will be to hold the big picture in mind at all times.

MANAGING INFORMATION

Information will be the currency of any successful organization.

You can access information from across the globe so easily with your fingertips in today's digital climate via a myriad of platforms with endless layers of content and knowledge.

You should filter out any irrelevant data which will simply cloud your judgement. In the same way that confusion will create chaos so clarity will make your understanding possible. You must, consequently, focus your attention on what will be important to you and those facts which will stimulate your ideas and shift your perspective. Do not become overwhelmed with information.

Distraction will be the enemy of your focus and your ability to think creatively. Be clear about your purpose in seeking information and do not become distracted or bogged down in complexity. Some information will, of course, need to be detailed if you are embarking on taking an important decision.

You may need to elicit the views of others in order to extract the information which you require and to challenge your own assumptions and alter your perspective. The views of your team-members can add value to your information-gathering activity. You must, however, be able to distinguish between information and fact when consulting another and be acutely aware that an opinion can be biased.

You must also consider different information packages and different reporting structures so that your data providers are effective and accurate. The selection of your information provider will, therefore, be critical for your organization – particularly those who provide financial data.

Do not fall into the trap of allowing your own bias to influence your judgement of the information which you receive. If you desire to find a given answer you may find that your filtering system will misinterpret data in order to attain the answer you desire. You may, for instance, distort data or delete information which you do not want to accept or to generalize too widely when considering your findings.

Gathering and interpreting information can often become an organic process for you. You might seek information about something simply because it may seem interesting and it could stimulate your curiosity but you should remember that information-gathering must fulfil your requirements. When you gather information it must serve a purpose and be of benefit. You will, therefore, need to objectively assess the value of the information which you receive before it can be utilized for the benefit of your corporate enterprise.

HUMAN RELATIONSHIPS

What tribes are is a very simple concept that goes back 50 million years. It's about leading and connecting people and ideas.

Seth Godin

FRUITFUL RELATIONSHIPS

Your ability to develop fruitful relationships will determine your level of success because everything in your organization will, at some level, depend on a relationship.

Quality relationships will be the fuel which will keep your organization afloat. The nature of a relationship will determine the quality and the effectiveness of your organization.

Fruitful relationships will be built on your ability to communicate effectively. What you convey or you omit to say will leave an impression on those you are addressing and those whom you meet.

People must buy into a relationship before they buy your service or product. Every individual will need to buy into your narrative in order to assess your integrity, character and motivation. Your associates will, hence, invest in you and your vision.

A fruitful relationship will create the medium through which your vision can be delivered and actioned. You should, therefore, deepen your understanding of the way in which a fruitful relationship can be developed swiftly.

> *A hairdresser will develop a relationship with his clients. Before we buy into the haircut we must buy into the hairdresser. The nature and depth of the relationship will determine the level of influence possible.*

FRUITFUL CULTURES

Your organization's values will influence its corporate culture. If you develop a healthy organizational culture you will create a successful business venture.

If your organization's ethos is healthy you will develop healthy corporate values. If your corporate culture is healthy you will encourage your personnel to be thoughtful, meticulous and industrious.

You should not fail to grasp the importance of encouraging your team to participate fully in developing a culture of betterment in your organization. Ideally you should strive to create a corporate environment in which every team-member will be actively seeking to improve the overall efficiency, effectiveness and experience of the organization and those employed by it.

If you can create a workable and efficient organizational structure you will generate a general attitude by which your personnel will operate. You should, for instance, always welcome a new team-member into your organization and you must encourage your colleagues to adopt a similarly supportive stance.

If your organization's interaction is unhealthy, on the other hand, your personnel will become adversarial and combinative. You should, therefore, stamp out any form of bullying culture or a culture in which one organizational sector considers itself superior to another.

You should note the tonal language of your personnel in order to decipher the culture within various sectors of your organization. You should consider, for instance, whether your senior team-members are addressing staff as if they were children rather than adults. There should be no room for parent-like or child-like behaviour within your organization which will damage your corporate culture.

If your internal environment ever becomes sterile then this culture may affect each employee's performance. You must, therefore, ensure that you banish any office-politics games in your organization. There should not be a rift between your executive staff and your personnel because this culture will not be conducive to working towards your vision.

Your industry itself can have a pre-existing culture and a correspondingly unwholesome reputation. Your sales team, for instance, may be inclined to put emphasis on hitting their targets at any cost and this culture will become ingrained into the fabric of your organization unless you can change it radically.

> *Your organization's culture will be like a tribe. If the tribe can work together it will out-think and out-perform the other tribes. The tribe will reflect the spirit of its members which will comprise the organization from the very top downwards.*

FORESIGHT

You should be perceived by your team as being able to predict the future with intuitive insight and logic even though there can be no actual certainty.

You will need to keep a track of trends so that you can make an educated prediction about the future and you can then forecast circumstances accordingly.

When you are forecasting for the future you should be taking a calculated risk based on your perception of future trends and your organizational needs. You may frequently find that corporate predictions and forecasts will be based on exploring and seizing opportunities which have been created by your consumers and by market trends.

Your experiences today will have been brought about by yesterday's decisions. If you assess the progress which your organization has made over its lifetime you can normally easily pinpoint certain events which have influenced the focus and the direction taken by your organization subsequently.

> *A ship's captain will assume that he will reach his destination with his cargo intact. He would know where the ship had to stop to refuel. The captain would know where his crew should place their nets advantageously. He would know how to avoid certain hazards while on his voyage.*

INSPIRATION

Inspiration will be the key ingredient for creating aspiration. Inspiration will entail infusing an idea into the mind of your associates.

Inspiration will generate an internal desire so that your personnel will want to emulate that aspiration in order to achieve and to pursue your objective. When you can inspire another you will ultimately create the idea that change is possible and desirable.

Inspiration will also be a provocation which will stimulate your team's aspirations and will engender an inbuilt desire to act constructively and spontaneously.

If you can inspire your team by your actions and your language-usage you will create a shift in the perception of your team-members.

Your function will be to appeal to the emotive responses, imagination and aspirations of your team-members in order to ignite the spark which will illuminate their souls. You should, therefore, talk positively, persuasively and passionately about your team, your colleagues and your organization in order to be purposefully driven towards success. Always ensure that you are interested in others and then seek feedback from your team so that you can become a model for others to automatically follow.

When you inspire your team your investment in terms of time and energy will be less costly than endeavouring to motivate them.

You will need to develop skills which will enable you to inspire those around you without undue effort. You can develop this skill by simply accepting that you are unique and that you already have a genuine talent to inspire others.

If you try too hard and endlessly rehearse your inspirational speech you may find that your audience will usually see through your tactics. By merely softening the tone of your voice and speaking with conviction you will be a natural inspiration to your team. If you have heartfelt passion you will inspire others by just being true to yourself and enhancing your self-belief.

Inspiration will derive from giving yourself a licence to be yourself. If you can simply be excited and you can allow others to share in your degree of enthusiasm you will engage your team effortlessly.

> *Music can stimulate an individual to move or dance in a given way according to the style, rhythm, pitch and tone.*

MOTIVATION

You should promote an ethos of motivation in your organization by stimulating your team-members into action by your encouragement.

Intrinsic motivation will occur when one of your team-members spontaneously engages in an activity because of the pleasure and reward which he will derive from his own action.

Extrinsic motivation must be fostered and nurtured externally in order to spur your team-member into action. You may, therefore, need to provide the stimulus which will provoke your personnel into action. You might need to dangle the carrot of a reward for success or, alternatively, you might persuade your team-member against inaction.

If your team-member is outcome-driven then he will need to appreciate the value of the outcome and the high probability of a successful result. You must, of course, motivate your personnel in order to ensure that each contributor will meet your objectives and fulfil your expectations.

Your team-members will, of course, need to see the significance of their actions in order to be fully motivated. When a team-member can understand a good reason for his action then his motivation may change from extrinsic desire to an intrinsic drive. You will need to ensure that you can motivate your personnel with a sufficient level of potency in order to initiate motivation.

Motivating your team can be a costly activity in terms of your time, energy and strategic planning. If you invest your personal resources into motivating a given team-member you will need to be sure that your efforts will be adequately rewarded. Some of your team-members will, of course, require more stimulation than others but always ensure that these personnel will be worth your investment.

If you can validate your team's effort each member of your team should then become even more incentivized by your praise and your personal validation of his efforts. If possible you should delegate the day-to-day running of your organization to your team.

Once your team fully understands your objective, your action plan is firmly in place and your team is correctly positioned then you will only need to observe, monitor and encourage. Positive reinforcement will also improve your team's performance. The ideal will be for you to watch your team go forth fearlessly and with joy. From this vantage point you can also look to the future.

Consider the motivational rewards which you can offer in order to motivate others. Money will only motivate those who lack creativity and are engaged in repetitive tasks.

> *Motivation will be helping someone to row while inspiration will be teaching someone to catch the wind and sail.*

TEAMWORK

TEAM CONSTRUCTION

You will need to appreciate the value of having a strong team at your disposal.

When the right collective of individuals is brought together and developed into a cohesive and synchronized team it will become a formidable force. Such a team can evolve organically but usually your team will need to be engineered.

Your ideal will be to create a team in which every individual will know his function and the way in which he can make a valuable contribution to the whole enterprise. You must, therefore, select your team with care in order to reflect your organizational needs. When you construct your team you will need to plan meticulously and not be forced into acting impulsively. Each of your team-members should possess the right skills and the ability to relate and interact with others in your team.

When your team is brought together for a short-term project your team-members may need to be able to work unaided and to co-operate fully with others in order to rapidly create a working culture characterised by efficiency and a sense of urgency.

If your team is working on a longer-term on-going project then your team-members must function collectively and with a cohesive ethos in order to be able to develop a joint-development initiative and to undertake long-term planning.

When constructing your team you will also need to consider the nature of its work. You must appreciate, for example, whether your team will be concerned primarily with volume output or the quality of a service.

If possible a number of teams can be brought together in order to deal with different aspects of your organization's work so that you can create a cross-cultural ethos of shared vision and healthy juxtaposition.

You might consider building a corporate team structure, for instance, in which several teams share resources and adopt matrix-management systems so that each team can function with minimal supervision.

A newly constructed team will require time to gel and to come together as one unit and you should strive to ensure that your team functioning can become clear and transparent in an open-framework environment in the pursuit of excellence.

> *A great conductor will turn his back on the audience and will lose himself in what he and his orchestra are doing. The conductor will enjoy the journey when every orchestral member in in harmony.*

TEAM DEVELOPMENT

You must understand your team-members in order to be able to develop your team.

If you can comprehend the way in which each of your team-members think you will be well placed to motivate your team. You will, therefore, need to identify the proportion of critical, constructive and creative thinkers in your team. Ideally your team should consist of team-members with a range of thinking capabilities so that thinking styles can be blended and will become complementary. You should, of course, discourage any rigid thinking on the part of your team-members.

A team which consists of personnel with a range of thinking styles will share a common vision and will develop the appropriate sense of urgency in order to meet their deadline. Your principal team-members should be selected very carefully because these team-members will then, in turn, need to select their own personnel.

Your team must also think and act collectively which will mean that each team-member must be able to think independently as well as being able work within the team's framework.

Your team must be characterized by mutual trust in order to become self-supporting, committed and sustainable. Your team-members, therefore, must be open and transparent.

Your team should also be able to pool its skill-set by recognizing and utilizing the strengths of individual members. Your team-leaders should be capable of managing this task efficiently.

If you conduct a team-appraisal system, a team-workshop or a team-building exercise you can usually mould your team into adopting your working policy.

Every team-member must be able to withstand challenge and he should not permit any inherent weakness to cloud his judgement and impartiality. You must also provide each team-member with a safe sanctuary in which to deal with delicate issues in connection with his function.

Your team must be given a clearly defined objective which all team-members can comprehend and achieve. You must, therefore, provide your team with objectives in context and show the relevance of your requirements.

> *A captain of a cruise liner cannot be spending his time in the engine room. He must oversee the entire operation of his ship and tend to his paying guests.*

TEAM HARNESSING

Once you have constructed your team as a unit you should harness your team's collective expertise so that it will work for you in a symbiotic relationship.

You must initially decide what your team will need to undertake and to accomplish. You may want your team, for instance, to process volumes of information or to apply specialist technical skills to a process.

The structure of your team must have a purpose and must add value to your enterprise. Streamlining the work of your team and enabling team-members to be effective and efficient will help you to ensure that your organization can be lean and strong. Your team's performance should be working as a unit in order to improve cumulative output in terms of quality and volume.

Your team's objective should always be underpinned by adequate preparation and planning and for this stage you may need to provide a degree of directional input. A clear mandate from you may, in some cases, be sufficient in order to allow your team to plan and execute its mission.

The better prepared your team will be the greater will be its success. Your team should also understand this principle because it could be the difference between success and failure.

Effective communication between your team-members will be essential if a successful outcome is to be forthcoming. You must, therefore, specify what must be communicated and to whom within your team as well as outlining the definitive lines of communicating in order to keep all personnel in the loop. Communication between key personnel will ensure that information will be to hand when required and in the appropriate form.

If your personnel desire problem-solving and solution-finding opportunities then you will need to alter your motivational tactics because challenge and accomplishment will not be the primary driving force in these circumstances.

> *A client worked in a tough retail environment where he had to constantly drive his employees to get the job done. What this client realized was that as soon as he stopped applying pressure his employees would stop trying.*
>
> *On one occasion this client was asked to step in so that he could cover for the manager while he was on holiday. When being briefed the client noticed how calm and easy-going the existing manager was and how respectful his staff were towards him. While talking to this manager the client realized that if he became approachable and likeable his staff would go out of their way to assist him.*

COMMUNICATION

Communication is a skill that you can learn. It's like riding a bicycle or typing. If you're willing to work at it you can rapidly improve the quality of every part of your life.

Brian Tracy

COMMUNICATION TODAY

The world of business has been transformed in many ways over the last 25 years. Modes of communication have evolved into emails, texts, tweets, emoji and phone calls.

Such changes will call for a different dialogue from you and you will need to be sensitive to the words and images which you utilize when communicating with others.

> *Communication ability consists of 55% body language, 38% tone of voice and 7% the actual words you use.*

WRITTEN COMMUNICATION

You should master the use of today's written communication medium and its implications.

You must learn to utilize the vast array of communication channels available today because the world is changing in the way in which it communicates. You will need to be ahead on the curve and should learn from those who are already integrated into today's communication system.

You should be mindful of the fact that while electronic communication can be extremely useful it can also be highly problematic. Once you have sent an electronic message you will have lost control of it forever. You cannot, for instance, decide who will have access to it. You should, therefore, carefully consider the content of your message and the delivery methods which you employ. You cannot guarantee that the information contained in your message will remain secure.

You must, consequently, treat any important and sensitive communication with caution and care. When you reveal your strategic action plans, for instance, it might be more expedient for you to convey such information face-to-face rather than risk committing it to the ether.

You could devise a set of communication rules for yourself. When you send a message, for instance, you could ask yourself a number of searching questions:

Is this the best way to convey my message?

Could my communication be dealt with by phone?

Why am I sending this email?

Will it be necessary to copy or blind copy others?

The way in which you deliver your communication will also be a message in itself. The form of your communication medium, therefore, will embed itself in your message and will create a symbiotic relationship between your message and the medium which delivers it.

If your communication is important then your medium must be appropriate. If your message is *Be strong and strive* then do not, for instance, deliver your communication to your team on flimsy paper with a cheap and fragile plastic ballpoint-pen.

An email, moreover, will have no voice yet your recipient can infer your attitude. You should, therefore, use words which will create the right impression in your recipient's mind. Your message should be kept concise while your delivery should be clear and unambiguous.

VERBAL COMMUNICATION

You should master the use of today's verbal communication medium and its implications.

You can only convey your message by telephone, for instance, effectively using your words, vocal volume, speech rhythm, vocal pitch and tonality. When making a phone call, consequently, you will need to give your message some advanced thought. You should consider your vocal tonality because you will not be able to see your recipient's reaction to your message. You will not have body language to assist you in conveying your message and there will be no eye-contact for you to monitor.

With a face-to-face meeting, however, you will need to consider your appearance and your demeanour as well as your vocal characteristics.

COMMUNICATION LANGUAGE

The language which you employ for all your communications must be thought through carefully. The questions which you might ask and the instructions which you will give should be well-formed.

Negative language will misdirect your recipient's attention and will, consequently, result an unwanted outcome. Common errors will occur, for example, when you employ negative words, such as *why*, *can't*, *try* and *should*.

Notice where your recipient's mind will be directed with this verbal exchange:

QUESTION   Why did the shipment get missed?

RESPONSE   Because the shipping docket was not ready in time.

The response which you have obtained in this conversation will bring the situation no further forward for you. You will remain in the problem-frame without a solution.

You could, however, ask your question differently in order to find a solution to the impasse:

QUESTION   What would need to happen for the shipment to get expedited today?

RESPONSE   I would need to get the transport manager to go to the office and manually print the docket for immediate shipment.

CONCLUSION   Great! Let me know when it's done.

A more probing question will thus lead your recipient's mind towards finding a solution for you.

EFFECTIVE COMMUNICATION

You should appreciate the way in which your recipient will receive your communication in order to get your message across effectively.

You should also consider the way in which you will convey your message in terms of your tone of voice, posture, speed of delivery and vocal volume when conveying information face-to-face.

Perhaps you could consider whether your recipient will respond by pictorial thought or by an emotive reaction. Every individual will have a preferred means of processing information which he has received. Your recipient will process information received by accessing one of his five sensory systems as a Representational System.

The visual system

The visual system will enable your recipient to process information with his sight.

The auditory system

The auditory will enable your recipient to process information with his hearing.

The kinaesthetic system

The kinaesthetic system will enable your recipient to process information with his touch or by emotive responses.

These Representation Systems of human information processing will influence your recipient at a neurological level. You can, therefore, benefit from understanding the communication mechanism adopted by your recipient and act appropriately.

If you listen carefully to what your correspondent says you will then be able to detect his main information processing medium. An individual will often reveal his preferred representational system in his own use of language:

VISUAL	I see what you mean
AUDITORY	I hear what you are saying
KINAESTHETIC	I feel that strongly

You can now decipher the way in which your correspondent will receive your message and you can assess the likely impact and his response. You can, by this means, become an effective communicator and you will empower yourself in the process.

Part of your remit will be to keep your organization and its personnel informed of the various activities in which your enterprise will be engaged.

You will, therefore, need to find the best way of communicating your thoughts so that your message can be digested and understood by your correspondent. Your message should be tailored to take account of your recipient's attention-span and his boredom-threshold. If your recipient's attention-span is short and his boredom-threshold is high you will need to consider this factor and act accordingly.

VISIONARY COMMUNICATION

If you are a visionary leader you will perceive great things and you must crucially communicate your vision clearly to your stakeholders which could prove surprisingly challenging.

Usually when you wish to put across a complex point you should adopt a pictorial representational approach. If you utilize pictorial images then you can convey thousands of words and facts in one image. Words alone may be confusing and ambiguous as well as tedious for your audience to absorb when you are communicating complex matter.

> *When an organization was surveyed the management discovered that only 40% of their employees understood the company vision and strategy. Yet once a pictorial representation was shown to these employees that percentage increased to over 90% which is a massive increase and one that needs to be emulated.*

MOTIVATIONAL COMMUNICATION

Your communication should inspire, motivate and propel your recipient into action. You will, of course, frequently need to convey your message with subtly in order to present your request so that it can have the desired effect.

If you are delivering facts, for instance, then this data should be presented creatively. When you are forced to present cold and hard evidence or to hammer home a difficult point then this should be done with conviction but without being tedious. You cannot rely on raw facts alone as a call-to-action order for your personnel.

INFLUENTIAL COMMUNICATION

Your message must impact on your recipient's thinking forcefully and completely. Your message, therefore, must influence your recipient's mind in order to generate your intended outcome.

A communication strategy could be useful for you in order to allow you to understand the information which should be disseminated to your stakeholder-groups. A communication strategy will also enable you to formulate the way in which messages can be managed in order to deliver the required influence.

The aim of all communication should be to direct your recipient's attention towards something meaningful and to alter his perspective on receipt of the message.

You should appreciate that your message will only have value in terms of what your recipient actually receives and not simply what you have conveyed. When addressing your team, for instance, you should remember that before you can influence others you must engage with your audience. If your audience is not concentrating then your message will not get through.

The world has become filled with information which has been designed to highjack your recipient's attention and to divert his focus. If your audience is being continually subject to endless distractions – phone calls, emails, text, pings and bleeps – then your communication will probably not capture your recipient's attention fully.

If you desire to influence your team you must develop a relationship with all team-members which will facilitate your influence. You must, consequently, reflect on your relationship with your audience and then consider your message accordingly.

APPROPRIATE COMMUNICATION

Your streamlined messages will be incomprehensible if they are not delivered in context. A message in its context will provide your recipient with his reason for action.

You will need to give serious thought to the appropriateness of your communication. You must make sure that the broad view has been set before you construct and deliver your message.

Once you have harnessed your thinking the next important stage will be for you to communicate that thinking to others. You will need to communicate to many people on various levels throughout your leadership career.

It will, consequently, be important for you to create some personal rules for yourself in order to avert potential disaster. You will have heard nightmare stories of leaked emails, misdirected text messages, compromising voice messages left on the wrong person's phone and letters sent to people with inappropriate information. Consider whether you are compromising yourself and risking sending your information to the wrong place at all times.

SOLUTION-FOCUSED COMMUNICATION

Communicating your message clearly and effectively will be paramount if you are to become a great leader. You will need to move away from problem-focused communication toward solution-focused dialogue. This will mean that you must move away from questions which consider the problem and move your questioning towards finding a solution.

The wrong question will make the answer irrelevant. A problem-focused question will usually seek to attribute blame or to reaffirm what you may already know about the situation.

A solution-focus question will endeavour to find a solution which can happen:

What would you like to have happen?

What needs to happen here?

What would help you to overcome this?

What are the smallest number of steps you could take which would make the biggest difference?

Can I help in some way so that you can accomplish this?

CONCISE COMMUNICATION

Your recipient will probably want his instructions to be direct with no nonsense and so you should get to the point, be concise, accurate, unambiguous and, most importantly, deliver your message sincerely. You will, in many ways, need to deliver your message as you would personally wish to receive it.

If you are not thoroughly conversant with your subject-matter you may begin to waffle. If you are not familiar with your audience you may similarly over-compensate by making paragraphs out of sentences.

VISUAL COMMUNICATION

The mind's ability to translate words into pictures will be hardwired.

If you utilize visual imagery you will enable the recipient of your communication to comprehend your message. You should appreciate, therefore, that your recipient's mind will translate your message from the written or the spoken word into visual images. The more accurate your recipient's pictorial representation the greater will be his clarity in comprehending your message.

You should take time to construct your messages with rich visual images and visually oriented words which can easily be accepted by your recipient.

METAPHORICAL COMMUNICATION

A metaphorical communication can be a visual inroad into your recipient's mind.

If you tell an allegorical story you will conjure up images in your recipient's mind from which he can draw a comparison. You should, of course, never explain your metaphorical story because it should be your recipient who must interpret its meaning and significance appropriately.

You will often be able to convey a highly complex concept with an analogy or a metaphor so that your communicant can absorb it effortlessly. You should, therefore, build up a catalogue of stories and metaphors so that you can aid your recipient's comprehension and minimize his level of resistance to any of your requests.

Suppose your core message was that you must get through the next quarter with reduced resources and without the support which you would ordinarily have at your disposal. By telling a team-member that he will need to cut back and he must work harder may cause discontent which could result in dissent. You could, however, frame your message as if it were a story about success.

> *Think about the great exploits of a group of airmen who survived for 11 days in the open seas in 1943 with just a sunk U-boat. With no supplies these airman found ways of surviving by utilizing their shirts as sails, using their handkerchiefs to collect rainwater and creating a fishing-net by altering their undergarments. This team came home to a hero's welcome.*

DECISION-MAKING

Perception is real even when it is not reality.

Edward de Bono

DECISION-MAKING PROCESSES

There will be a range of basic decisions which you must make on a daily basis for which little forethought will be required. Your decision-making process may, alternatively, demand that you select from a number of different options.

Your decision can be to take action or to remain inactive. A decision to take action will move you from one situation to another while a choice to remain inactive will allow you to continue along your current path.

You will take decisions which are rooted in your values, principles and standards of behaviour. What you value will inform your decision-making and will provide the framework for the way in which you will select a path of action.

Your value-judgement will dictate the outcome and the risk involved in making a decision. Your thinking powers and your thinking styles will govern your motivation and, consequently, the result of the outcome. When you take both routine and complex decisions, therefore, you should make positive choices some of which will become instinctive rather than analytic.

COMPETENCE

When you acquire your leadership skills you will transit a number of distinct learning phases from being inept to becoming proficient. You can apply a competence formula, therefore, to all your decision-making.

Unconscious incompetence

During the initial stage of unconscious incompetence you will have an awareness of what will be required.

If your leadership activity might be exploring foreign territory, for instance, then you will not have grasped the subtleties and the intricacies of this new venture enough to take an informed decision. You may, therefore, encounter several blind spots because of insufficient information or a lack of awareness of the situation.

Conscious incompetence

You will next enter the stage of conscious incompetence in which you will know what will be required even though you may not be proficient enough yet. You may, at this stage, need to summon an expert in order to assist you in a given area so that you can take an informed decision.

Conscious competence

At the conscious competence stage you will have acquired your leadership skill but you will still need to remain focused and attentive. Your decision-making process will not be an automatic competence.

Unconscious competence

The final stage of unconscious competence will be the ideal in which you will function with a degree of fluency and ease with little conscious thought when you take decisions.

You will internalize the pattern of your skill and can apply it without any analytic thought processes. While this stage of ease and comfort can be stress-free you should, of course, be wary of allowing yourself to stagnate when taking decisive action.

DECISION-DRIVERS

Your decisions can be driven either by desire or by fear according to what drives you to make a decision. The intention behind your decision will govern your motivation and will, in turn, dictate the outcome.

If your intention is driven by desire then you will maximize your opportunities by moving in the right direction. If your decision, however, is driven by fear then the result may not be ideal because you may be moving away from your target by trying to safeguard yourself.

You may find that you are forced into taking a decision because of circumstances which are anxiety-provoking and so you will take a decision based on fear. If your organization gets into financial difficulty, for instance, you may be forced to make a difficulty choice and will, consequently, feel under pressure and disempowered. You cannot afford to fall prey to a fearful situation if you are to thrive. You may need to refocus your perspective in order to view the situation as a positive opportunity for change when making a decision.

You will find that sometimes a decision will call for a group-discussion – perhaps for political or democratic reasons. If a unanimous decision can easily be reached by the group then this route will be serviceable. If protracted negotiations ensue then this situation can result in an unworkable compromise merely so that the decision can be taken. Dissenters in a compromise will then not be the most effective supporters of the decision and its ramifications.

You must also guard against allowing your organization to keep the status quo because group decision-makers prefer the safe option rather than voting for implementing change.

When you consider decision-making you should become aware that every decision retains a value. Where there is no value there will be no reason for you to act and hence no reason for you to take any initiative.

There will be value in the decisions you take as well as value in the outcome of your choices and any knock-on effects of your consequent action.

You must also comprehend the value of your thinking-flexibility and your decision-making skill supported by information provision so that your organization can thrive. Your decisions should, therefore, be based on an evaluation of a situation in terms of its value and the power of your value-judgements. You should as far as possible employ creative thinking skills when taking a decision so that you can make a sound judgement as well as critical thinking in order to assess the factual information.

DECISION-MAKING VALUES

When you are assessing and establishing values you will need to set these ideals in context so that you can reap the benefits.

Human values

Human values deal with human emotive responses and the consequences to the people affected by any decisions you take. Your team must be able to support your decisions with conviction and, therefore, each team-member must wholeheartedly believe in the cause.

Organizational values

Organizational values are those to which your organization will be committed in order to service its personnel and its clientele and so that you can retain equality and fairness for all.

Quality values

Quality values are those by which your organization's integrity will be measured regardless of whether your enterprise is offering a product or a service.

Creative values

Creative values will involve those aspects of your enterprise which will require innovative thinking styles for improving performance and efficiency.

Environmental values

Environmental values will be concerned with the effect of your decision-making on the culture and the climate of your organization and the market for its products and services.

Perceptual values

Perceptual values will be the substance of what your team will perceive as having a benefit. If your personnel feel secure without any threat, for instance, then your team will be fulfilled in the workplace, self-motivated and committed to the task in hand.

Organizational values

Organizational values are those to which your organization itself will be committed. These are usually based upon people, clients, equality and fairness. The value to your organization will be to create an environment which generates a sense of belonging and spawns a highly motivated workforce.

If an organization has an uncared for workforce or a neglected client group there will probably be an unenthusiastic team driving the business and a diminishing client list. It makes sense to ensure that healthy human values are accepted and embedded within your organizational values.

Not all organizations strive for the same thing. Values sought can vary. Financial values, for instance, versus community-based values are significantly distinct.

In a corporation, for instance, you must to focus your attention on organizational values and you must accept that your decisions will be fundamentally driven by sustainability and growth.

You might, consequently, ask yourself:

Is the production delivering a product that can be sold at a profit?

Are the products in keeping with market needs and pricing?

Is the mechanism to deliver the products to the market the best value available?

Is the marketing of the products adding value to the demand?

A different set of questions would apply to a government department or an enterprise offering a service.

DEPLOYING RESOURCES

The medium is the message.

Marshall McLuhan

RESOURCE MANAGEMENT

Your tactical resources will consist of the sum total of all your assets as the fuel which will drive your enterprise towards realizing your vision. You must have a keen awareness of the resources at your disposal so that each can be effectively deployed and none will be wasted.

Your tangible resources will consist of your wealth, financial reserves and human resources while your personal resources will comprise your time, energy, perceptual agility, thinking style, personal attributes and communicative ability.

TIME

Time can be considered as a value in terms of how long it might take you to accomplish a given task, when to seize an opportune moment and the cost of the time invested.

Time is, however, not a renewable source because once it has been spent it will be gone forever.

You will, of course, need to quantify time as a value by making the most economical use of it. Time, of course, can easily slip through the fingers of your personnel and yet each second wasted will collectively accumulate into a significant amount.

Consider your relationship with time as if it were an entity with which you can interact and then assess whether your time-input will be worth the final outcome. If you enjoy the company of time then it may fly by and it may drag if your environment creates lethargy or life is tedious. Ask yourself whether you are normally aware of the passage of time and identify those occasions when you find yourself consulting the clock or you are pressurized into meetings.

Consider also whether your personnel are aware of time, whether a team-member tends to be too hasty or often behind schedule because he is out of rhythm.

You will need to perceive the cost of time if you are to prevent it from slipping away. Decide where you are going to allot your time as a resource based on your vision. A morning meeting, for instance, could be set for a thirty-minute slot so that visitors know that their time with you will, of necessity, be restricted.

You could, moreover, shorten a deadline for the delivery of a report from one of your team-members in order to focus his mind. If you tell him that he has twenty-four hours in which to submit his report then he may well use the whole of that amount of time whereas if you shorten the deadline he will respond accordingly.

Your timing can also be an instinctive and intuitive faculty when you select the right time to take action because you will have sufficient information to hand.

> *A client dreaded the thought of his monthly board meetings. Apparently this client hated having to listen to his fellow-directors giving their lengthy monthly reports which were already available on the organization's computer network for all to inspect.*
>
> *The client was then asked to restrict the time allotted to his fellow-directors for presenting their reports to fifteen minutes. By this means his fellow-directors managed to reduce their presentations down to five minutes.*

WEALTH

Wealth in the broadest sense will include finances, assets, intellectual property, commercial flexibility, time-saving costs, expertise and personnel with special skills.

You must have a good grip on your organization's financial position even though you may not have an in-depth knowledge of management accountancy. The interpretation of your monthly financial reports will be a skill which you must master so that you can assess your organization's profit-and-loss position and you can then track its forward course.

A competent financial director will be an essential commodity for you to be able to act with certainty because you will then know where you are and what you will need achieve.

You should appreciate that you must conserve your wealth and invest it wisely without being over-cautious so that it will not evaporate. You should not, of course, under-estimate the value of your personnel as an asset which will generate your organization's wealth.

Taking stock and evaluating the wealth available to you should become second nature to you.

VITALITY

You must have the energy and the stamina to keep going and not appear at any time to your team to be disinterested or unenthusiastic in your work. You must always seem to be fully charged and dynamic in the eyes of your personnel because your vitality will set the tone for your organization. Your vitality, enthusiasm and energy will be engaging and contagious.

You could visualize your vital resources as if they were a battery which needs to be regularly recharged and the recharge rate will vary according to the way in which you maintain your mind and body. Recharging your battery will naturally occur overnight when you mind and body will need adequate rest even while sorting out the day's problems. Do not neglect yourself or over-work yourself as this form of self-punishment will be counter-productive. Apply the formula that rest and recreation will result in rejuvenation for you.

EXPERTISE

Do not allow any special skills or expertise which your personnel may possess to lay dormant.

Your team-members must be invited to contribute whenever possible as a means of stimulating them. Be sure to bring out the best in your personnel, offer opportunities for advancement and constructively challenge a given team-member when necessary. You must, of course, know your team's strengths and weaknesses.

The skills and expertise of your personnel will be the life-blood of your organization. If a given team-member, for instance, excels in organizational skills, is able to infuse enthusiasm in others or has a keen sense of humour then applaud and exploit this natural ability.

If you can appreciate what motivates your team you will be able to inspire each team-member accordingly and time invested in this activity will reap rewards for you. Being mindful of the needs and aspirations of your personnel will create a sincere and positive rapport between you and this ethos can spread throughout your organization.

Any intelligent fool can make things bigger,
more complex, and more violent. It takes a
touch of genius – and a lot of courage – to
move in the opposite direction.

Albert Einstein

ABOUT THE AUTHOR

Georges Philips has worked with numerous executives in leadership positions across several corporate areas over the last 30 years.

Georges has assisted many leaders with a range of leadership issues and managerial transformation. Georges specializes in helping his clients to manage people in complex environments with corporate arbitration negotiations, coaching and mentoring skills.

Georges has also coached and trained countless individuals in neuro-linguistic programming, stress management, post-traumatic stress disorder, hypnotherapy and belief restructuring. As a certified Edward de Bono trainer Georges has assisted many individuals and teams to learn some of the most powerful thinking skills available. Much of this book is influenced by the simplicity and depth of Dr de Bono teachings.

Over the last 25 years Georges has worked independently with national and international organizations, such as Berenson, Bear Bank, Standard Bank, Nomikos Shipping, IHSS, the CEO office, the NHS, Savills Estate Agents and

Mitre Linen Services, in order to develop better communication skills and thinking processes which can empower his clients to inspire individuals and teams.

Georges has authored and co-written many books related to thinking styles and neuro-linguistic studies. His books include *Change Directions*, with the foreword by Edward de Bono, who is considered to be one of the world's greatest thinkers. George created the very successful *Gold Counselling*™ model - a complete therapeutic methodology which has been designed to restructure negative beliefs.

As a performance coach and mentor, Georges helps his clients to maximize potential and overcome problematic issues, such as presentation anxiety, fear of human confrontation, communication skills and other leadership issues.

For coaching, mentoring and consultancy with Georges Philips please visit www.georgesphilips.com or telephone 0208 446 2210.

FURTHER READING

Georges Philips (2011) *Change Directions: Perceive it, Believe it, Achieve it.*

Georges Philips & Tony Jennings (2016) *My Little Book of NLP.*

Georges Philips & Tony Jennings (2016) *My Little Book of Verbal Antidotes.*

Georges Philips & Lyn Buncher (2014) *Gold Counselling: Creative and Analytical Transformation.*

David McCandless (2012) *Information is Beautiful.*

Edward de Bono (2015) *Simplicity.*

Edward de Bono (2000) *Six Thinking Hats.*

Edward de Bono (2015) *Tactics: The Art and Science of Success.*

Jack Trout (2015) *Trout on Simplicity.*

Jack Trout (2001) *The Power Of Simplicity: A Management Guide to Cutting Through the Nonsense and Doing Things Right.*

Malcolm Gladwell (2009) *Outliers: The Story of Success.*

Malcolm Gladwell (2006) *Blink: The Power of Thinking Without Thinking.*

Stephen R Covey (2004) *The Seven Habits of Highly Effective People.*

John Kotter & Holger Rathgeber (2006) *Our Iceberg is Melting: Changing and Succeeding Under any Conditions.*

John Kotter (2008) *A Sense of Urgency.*

Joseph O'Connor & Ian McDermott (2004) *An Introduction to NLP: Psychological Skills for Understanding and Influencing People.*

Paul Arden (2003) *It's Not How Good You Are, It's How Good You Want to Be.*

Jim Collins (2001) *Good To Great.*

Daniel Goleman (1996) *Emotional Intelligence: Why It Can Matter More Than IQ.*

Mark H McCormack (2014) *What They Don't Teach You at Harvard Business School.*

Seth Godin (2007) *The Dip: The Extraordinary Benefits of Knowing When to Quit (and When to Stick).*